Ragbag

Written by Joanne Reay
Illustrated by Kathi Ember

There once was a rat called Ragbag.
Ragbag had a plan.
There once was a cat called Fat Cat.
Fat Cat had a can.

And with the can, away Ragbag ran.

Fat Cat had a hat.

And with the hat and the can,
away Ragbag ran.

Fat Cat had some jam.

And with the jam and the hat and the can, away Ragbag ran.

Fat Cat had a bat.

And with the bat and the jam and the hat and the can, away Ragbag ran.

Fat Cat had a mat.

SNATCH

And with the mat and the bat and the jam and the hat and the can, away Ragbag ran.

Fat Cat had a pan.

And with the mat and the bat and the hat and the jam and the can, Ragbag ran . . .

. . . into the pan!

Fat Cat had . . . a nap.